Date: 4/8/11

Maps

by Sally Hewitt

amicus

Published by Amicus
P.O. Box 1329, Mankato, Minnesota 56002

U.S. publication copyright © 2011 Amicus.
International copyright reserved in all countries.
No part of this book may be reproduced in any
form without written permission from the publisher.

Printed in the United States of America at Corporate
Graphics, in North Mankato, Minnesota.

Published by arrangement with the Watts Publishing
Group Ltd., London.

Library of Congress Cataloging-in-Publication Data
Hewitt, Sally.
  Maps / by Sally Hewitt.
    p. cm. -- (Starting geography)
  Includes index.
  Summary: "Discusses different types of maps,
  how they are used, and how they represent
  geographical areas. Includes hands-on activites"
  --Provided by publisher.
  ISBN 978-1-60753-126-5 (hardcover)
  1. Maps--Juvenile literature. 2. Map reading--
Juvenile literature. I. Title.
  GA105.6.H49 2011
  912--dc22
                                    2009023301

Editor: Katie Dicker
Art Direction: Dibakar Acharjee (Q2AMedia)
Designer: Shweta Nigam (Q2AMedia)
Picture researcher: Kamal Kumar (Q2AMedia)
Craft models made by: Shweta Nigam (Q2AMedia)
Photography: Tarang Saggar (Q2AMedia)

1211
32010

9 8 7 6 5 4 3 2 1

Picture credits:
t=top b=bottom c=center l=left r=right

Cover: Index Stock Imagery/Photolibrary
Title page: Pakhnyushcha/Shutterstock
Insides: Pakhnyushcha/Shutterstock: 6,
Bob Watkins/Alamy: 7tr, Sunnyside/Istockphoto: 7b,
Flashfilm/Getty Images: 8, Tersina/Dreamstime: 9tr,
John Carnemolla/Corbis: 9tc, Crackshots/Corbis: 12,
Nicoolay/Istockphoto: 13tr, Kycstudio/Istockphoto:
14, ImageZebra: 16, Mapoftheunitedstates.org: 17tr,
Courtesy of the University of Texas Libraries,
The University of Texas at Austin: 18bl, University
Of Buffalo, The State University Of New York: 18br,
Yuliyan Velchev/Shutterstock: 19tr, Richard T.
Nowitz/Corbis: 20b, MapXpert: 20bl, Chad
McDermott/Shutterstock: 22, Elisabeth
Munsterhjelm/Fotolia: 23c, Michel
Touraine/Jupiterimages: 24, Song_mi/Istockphoto:
25bl, Vova Pomortzeff/Alamy: 26,
Amorphis/Bigstockphoto: 27tr, Dmitry
Naumov/Shutterstock: 27tl, Bliznetsov/Shutterstock:
27tc, Felinda/Bigstockphoto: 27tb,
Kycstudio/Istockphoto: 27cl.
Q2AMedia Image Bank: Imprint page, Contents page,
9, 11, 15, 17, 19, 21.
Q2AMedia Art Bank: 10, 13, 21, 23, 25, 27.

With thanks to our model Shruti Aggarwal.

Every attempt has been made to clear copyright.
Should there be any inadvertent omission, please
apply to the publisher for rectification.

Contents

Words that appear in **bold** can be found in the glossary on pages 28–29.

What is a map?

A map is a drawing of a place. It usually shows the view as if you were looking down on a place from above. A map can be of the whole world, or just the street where you live.

Flattening Out

Earth is shaped like a ball. A map in the shape of a **globe** (right) gives us the most accurate picture of the world. A map on a piece of paper has to be flattened out to fit on the page. A book of maps is called an **atlas**.

A globe is slightly tilted. It spins the same way that Earth spins in space.

Finding the Way

When you are standing in a city surrounded by tall buildings, you can't see very far. A **street map** shows you the whole city so you can find where you are and where you want to go.

Planning a Route

A route map showing paths, roads, railroad lines, cities, and towns will help you plan a car trip, a bike ride, or a walk. A map will help you find the quickest way, without getting lost!

You can find street names, bus stations, parks, and buildings on a street map.

Hikers use a map to find paths to follow. Maps also show interesting features to look for.

Bird's-Eye View

Maps are drawn from a **bird's-eye view**. A bird's-eye view is what you see if you are looking down from above—just like a bird flying overhead. You can get a bird's-eye view from a tall building.

Higher and Higher

The higher you go, the bigger the area you can see. Roads and buildings look smaller as you climb higher. A map of a big area shows less detail than a map of a small area.

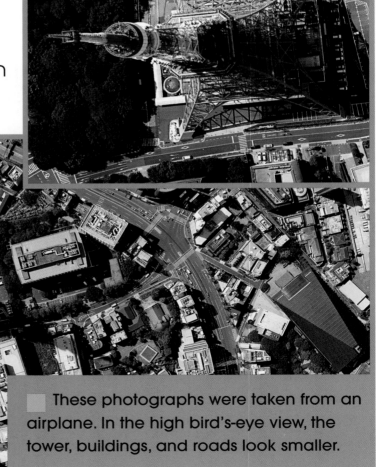

Low bird's-eye view

High bird's-eye view

These photographs were taken from an airplane. In the high bird's-eye view, the tower, buildings, and roads look smaller.

Looking Down

If you look straight down on an object or a place, it will look very different from how you usually see it. An **aerial view** shows the outline of different features, such as the bend of a river, a clump of trees, or the shape of buildings.

These pictures show Sydney Opera House from the ground and from the air.

Trick Your Friends With Bird's-Eye Views

You will need:
- 4 familiar objects (mug, lamp, boot, etc.)
- 4 pieces of card stock
- camera or markers • glue

1 Take a photograph (or draw a picture) looking straight down on each object. Stick your printed photo (or drawing) onto a piece of card stock.

2 Photograph (or draw) the same object from the side. Stick this image onto the other side of the card.

3 Can your friends guess the object from the bird's-eye view? Turn the card over to show them what it is.

Symbols

Maps have lots of **symbols** and colors. They help give detailed information on a map in a clear way. Lines show **boundaries**, roads, railroads, and rivers. Other symbols are letters or pictures.

A Key

A small chart tells you what all the symbols mean. It is called a **key** because it helps to "unlock" the map. Sometimes, picture symbols are easy to recognize. You may be able to spot a restaurant, a church, or a campsite, for example, without looking at the key.

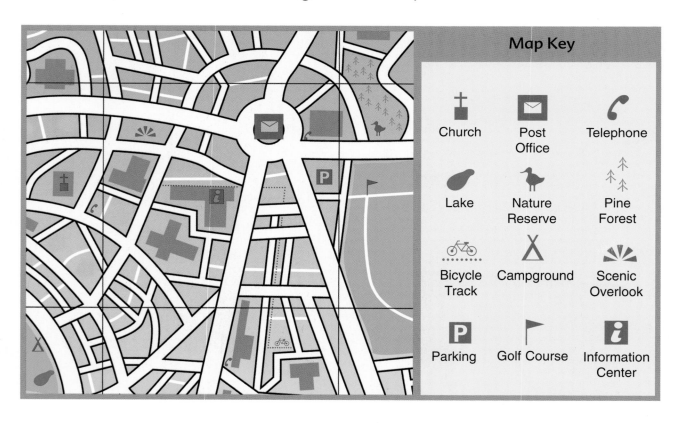

Play Match the Symbols

You will need:
- card stock • scissors
- road atlas
- colored pencils or markers

1 Cut the card stock into 20 or more playing-card-sized rectangles.

2 Find the page of symbols in your atlas. Copy a different symbol onto each card.

3 Deal the cards between two players. Place the piles face down in front of you.

4 Choose a page in the atlas. Take turns looking at the top card and finding the symbol on the map. Place the card on top of the symbol.

5 Not all the symbols will be shown on every page of your atlas. Discard the cards with symbols not shown on the map.

6 The winner is the player with the most matched symbols on the map.

Making Maps

Making maps is called **cartography**.
A cartographer collects measurements,
aerial photographs, and **satellite** images
sent from space. This information is fed
into computers to create accurate maps.

Up-to-date

Maps must be kept up-to-date. New roads
are built, cities grow in size, and countries
can change their names and boundaries.
An out-of-date map is very confusing!

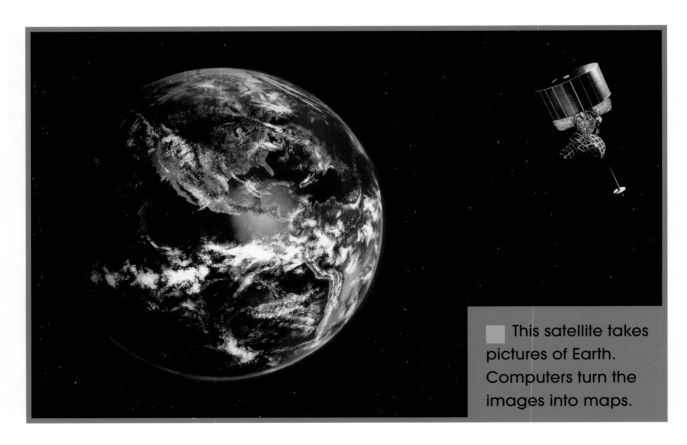

This satellite takes
pictures of Earth.
Computers turn the
images into maps.

Early Cartographers

Without the help of airplanes, satellites, and computers, it was difficult for early cartographers to make accurate maps. They had to draw what they saw from the ground. It took them a very long time.

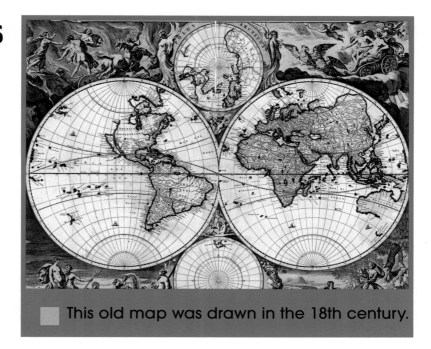

This old map was drawn in the 18th century.

Draw a Map of Where You Live

1 With an adult, go for a walk near your home or close to your school.

2 Make notes of what you see.

3 Start with your home or school in the middle of the page.

4 Draw a map of your area as accurately as possible (A).

5 Compare it with a printed street map (B). How accurate were you?

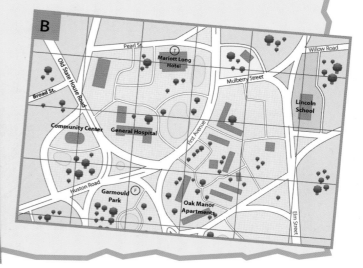

Compass Points

To find the way, we need to know what direction we are going. A **compass** helps us find the direction. The four main points of a compass are north, south, east, and west.

Finding Directions

A compass has a magnetic needle that always points to the north. North is always at the top of a map. The sun can also help you find your direction. Wherever you are on Earth, the sun always rises in the east and sets in the west.

On this compass you can see the main points (clockwise from the top): north, east, south, and west.

Eight-Point Compass

Sometimes we need more accurate directions to follow. For example, halfway between south and west is southwest (SW). A compass can be divided into eight points: N, NE, E, SE, S, SW, W, NW.

Make a Compass Treasure Hunt

You will need:
- 2 pieces of card stock (different colors) • scissors
- compass • markers • treasure (such as candy) • glue

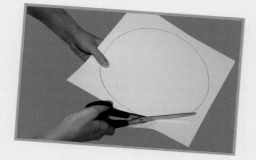

1 Cut one circle of card stock about the size of a dinner plate. Cut another circle about the size of a saucer.

2 Fold the circles in half, then in quarters, then in eighths. Open them. On each fold line, write the compass points on the edge of the big circle.

3 Glue the small circle onto the big circle with each line pointing to a compass point. Draw over the lines to make them stand out.

4 Lie your compass on the floor and use a real compass to find north. Face your compass in the same direction.

5 Hide some treasure.

6 Give your friend directions toward the treasure. For example, 2 steps N, 3 steps NE.

Map Lines

Lines are drawn on maps to help us measure distances and find places. On a world map, lines of **latitude** and **longitude** split the Earth into sections. On a smaller map, a **grid** system is used.

Latitude and Longitude

Lines of latitude run horizontally around Earth. They are measured in degrees from the **equator**. Lines of longitude run vertically around Earth, between the north and south **poles**.

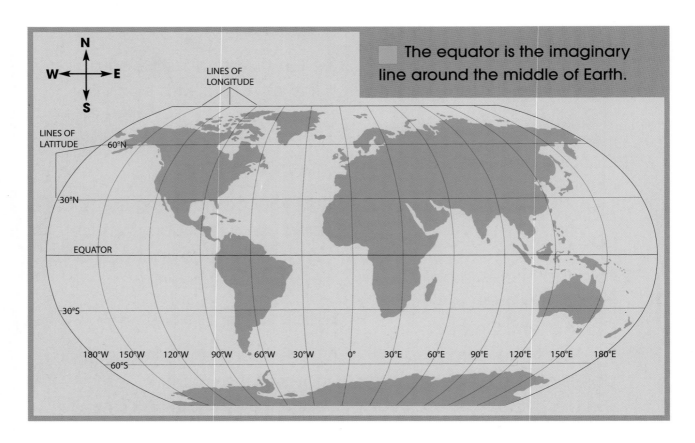

N
W ← → E
S

LINES OF LONGITUDE

The equator is the imaginary line around the middle of Earth.

LINES OF LATITUDE

60°N

30°N

EQUATOR

30°S

60°S

180°W 150°W 120°W 90°W 60°W 30°W 0° 30°E 60°E 90°E 120°E 150°E 180°E

Grids

A map of a smaller area, such as a town, is divided into squares to make a grid. Squares running across the page have letters. Squares running down the page have numbers. We use these letters and numbers to describe the location of each square.

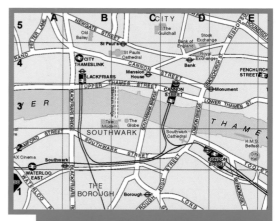

On this map, the HMS *Belfast* is in square E2.

Play Hunt the Symbol

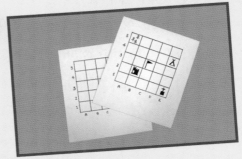

1 Draw 4 sets of grids with 5 x 5 squares, with each square measuring about ½ inch (1.5 cm). Label the squares A B C D E from left to right along the bottom and 1 2 3 4 5 up the side.

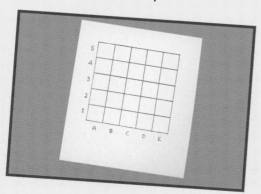

2 To play with a friend, take two grids each. Choose 5 map symbols (look at page 10 or a map for ideas).

On one of your grids, secretly draw each symbol in 5 different squares.

3 Take turns calling a position on the grid, such as "A2." If your opponent has put a symbol in that square, draw it in your blank grid. If not, put an X. The winner is the first to find all their opponent's symbols.

Scale

If maps were life-size, they would have to be enormous. Instead, maps are drawn to **scale**. This means that things are shown accurately but much smaller than they really are.

Scale

The scale on a map gives exact measurements. On the small-scale map (A), 1 inch on the map represents 5 miles on the ground. On the large-scale map (B), 1 inch on the map represents 0.25 miles on the ground.

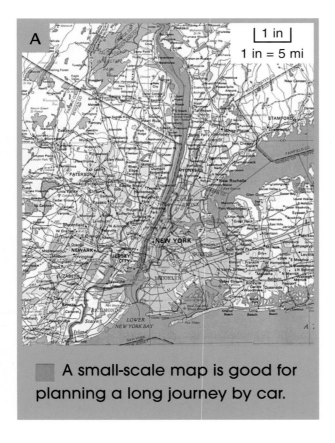

A small-scale map is good for planning a long journey by car.

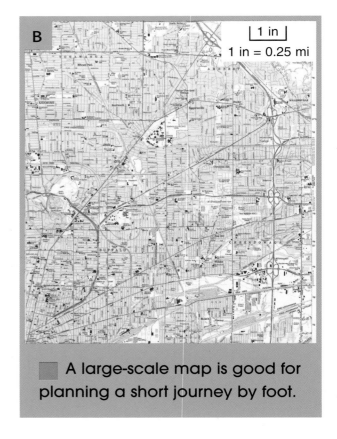

A large-scale map is good for planning a short journey by foot.

Shrink and Grow a Map!

You will need:
- 1 in x 1 in (2.5 cm x 2.5 cm) square of paper
- 6 in x 6 in (15 cm x 15 cm) square of paper
- pencil • ruler

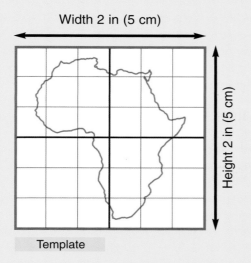

Width 2 in (5 cm)

Height 2 in (5 cm)

Template

1 Fold the pieces of paper in half, then in quarters. Unfold them. You will see four squares on each.

2 Copy the template map of Africa shown above onto the small paper to shrink the map. Draw a faint grid like the one shown to help you work out where to draw everything. Use your ruler to work out the distances of the map lines you draw.

Africa

Remember that the grid squares and distances will be half the size of the original template map.

3 Now copy the map onto the large piece of paper to grow it. Draw a faint grid again to help you. This time, the grid squares and distances will be three times the size of the original template map.

Landscapes

Maps are drawn on flat pieces of paper, but lines, colors, and symbols show us what the landscape looks like in real life. Areas of color and pattern show mountains, forests, deserts, and water.

Contour Lines

More detailed maps use **contour lines**, which are usually brown. A contour line joins the places on a map that are of equal height. When contour lines are drawn close together, they show steep slopes. When the lines are drawn further apart, they show flatter land.

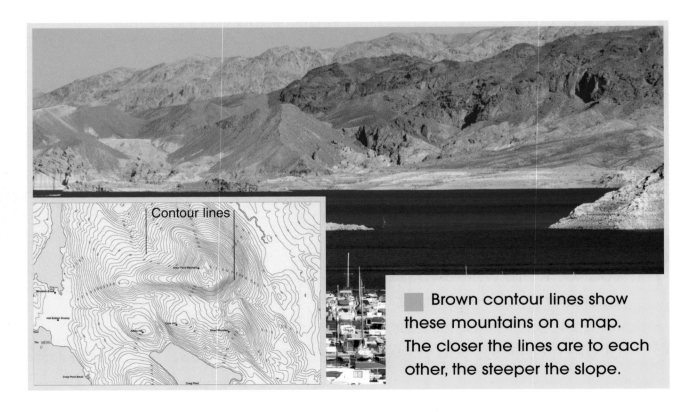

Contour lines

Brown contour lines show these mountains on a map. The closer the lines are to each other, the steeper the slope.

Make and Map a Landscape

You will need:
- small tray • foil • air-dry clay
- waterproof paint • sand
- water • paper • markers

1 Line the tray with foil.

2 Make an interesting landscape with clay. Include features such as mountains, hills, valleys, and a river.

3 Let the clay dry and then paint it. Add sand and water to your landscape. You could also add trees and bushes.

4 Draw an aerial view of your landscape and color the different features. What would a map of the landscape look like?

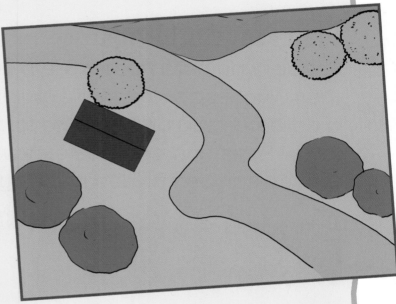

Plans

A plan is a simple drawing that represents a thing or a place. A plan helps us picture what something looks like. A map is a kind of plan.

Plans for Buildings

People who build houses use plans to help them. Architects design the building. They draw a detailed map of the house for the builders to follow. Pipes and cables are drawn on the plan so they can be installed in the right places.

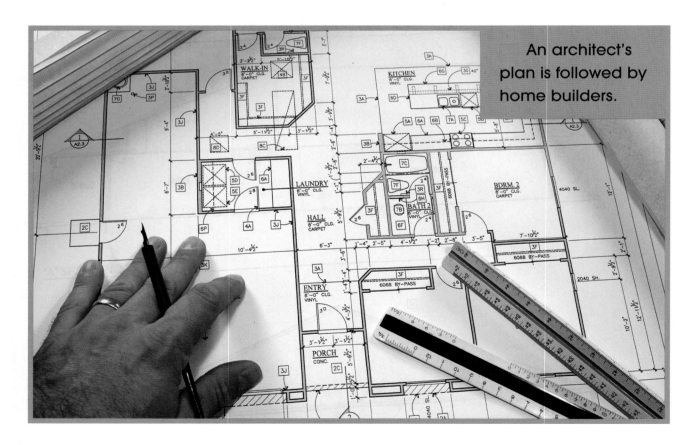

An architect's plan is followed by home builders.

Room Plans

Room plans are like simple maps. They are useful for deciding the best way to arrange furniture. Drawing a plan will help you to see if there is room for all the furniture to fit.

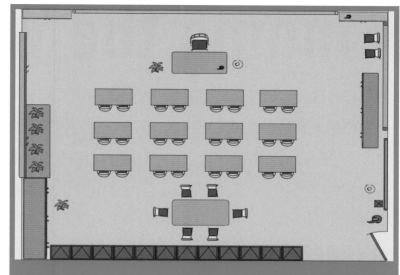

A classroom plan helps a teacher organize the desks and equipment.

Draw a Plan of Your Friend's Bedroom

1 With a friend, describe your bedrooms to each other.

2 Draw a plan from your friend's description. Draw details such as the shape of the room,

where the doors and windows are, and how the furniture is arranged.

3 Compare your plans to the actual rooms. How accurate are they?

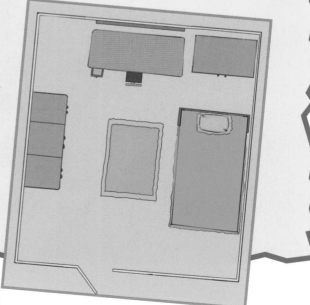

Finding the Way

When you go for a walk or a **hike**, take a map and a compass with you. A map will show you paths and **landmarks**, while a compass will tell you which direction to go.

Where am I?

First, find out where you are on your map, then look at where you want to go. Turn the map so that what you can see in front of you is also in front of you on the map. Watch for landmarks that are marked on the map.

When you go for a walk, checking a compass and a map will keep you going in the right direction.

Mark a Trail and Find Your Way

You can play this in a big yard, park, or playground with adults to help you.

You will need:
- 5 bags of colored playing chips (1 bag of red, 1 bag of blue, etc.) • pen • paper

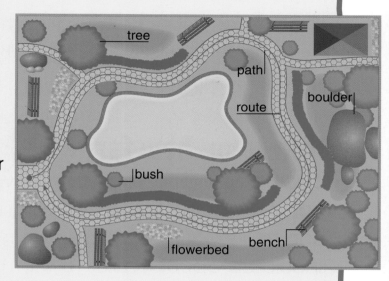

1 Plan a circular route with several landmarks such as a tree, a bench, a flower bed, a bush, or a boulder. Start and finish at the same point.

2 Leave the 5 bags of playing chips equally spaced along the route.

3 Draw a map of the route including the landmarks (but not the position of the bags!). Each player will need a copy of the map, so you will need to make a few copies.

4 To play the game, use the map to follow the trail. Pick up a different colored chip from each bag to prove you have found the way. The winner is the first to the finish with 5 different colored chips.

Planning a Walk

A walk can be a short stroll or a long hike that takes all day. A walk with friends is fun, but remember to take time to stop, listen, and look around you.

How long, how far?

Decide how long you want to walk for. If you can walk about 2 miles (3.2 km) in an hour and you want to walk for 2 hours, your route should be about 4 miles (6.4 km). Look at whether your route has flat or steep land.

A steep climb takes longer than a flat walk and can be more tiring.

Equipment

If you are going for a long walk, take water and a snack or a light picnic. Check the weather for the right clothes to wear and put on strong, comfy shoes or hiking boots.

☐ This is the type of equipment you will need for a walk on a warm, sunny day.

Plan a Walk

Plan a walk with your friends. Make a chart of features to spot (see below). Each time you see a feature, mark it with a star. Use a map to help you to find the places on your walk. Who can collect the most stars?

Walk in the Country		
Buildings	Church ✝ ****	Barn 🏚 **	Nature Center 🏠 *
Leisure	Picnic Site **** ⛱	Golf Course 🚩 *	Fishing 🐟 **
Nature	Pine Forest 🌲 *	Lake **	River ***
Convenience	Telephone *** 📞	Information Center * ℹ	Parking *** 🅿

Glossary

aerial view

An aerial view is the view you can see of an area from above, as from an airplane.

atlas

An atlas is a book of maps and information about places.

bird's-eye view

A bird's-eye view is the view of an area that a bird would see when flying.

boundary

A boundary is a line on a map that shows where one area of land is divided from another. Boundaries divide countries, states, and provinces, for example.

cartography

Cartography is the process of making maps. A cartographer is someone who makes maps.

compass

A compass helps you find directions. It has a magnetic needle that points to the north.

contour line

A contour line is a line on a map that joins together points of land that are the same height.

equator

The equator is the line on a map that marks the imaginary line around the center of Earth, halfway between the north and south poles.

globe

A globe is a ball with a map of the world printed on it.

grid

A grid is made up of lines that divide a map into squares. A grid makes it easier to find places on a map.

hike

A hike is a long walk in the country.

key

A key is the chart on a map that explains what the map symbols mean.

landmark

A landmark is a particular feature, such as a hill or a building.

latitude

Lines of latitude run across a map north and south of the equator.

longitude

Lines of longitude run down a map between the north and south poles.

poles

The north and south poles are the furthest points on Earth from the equator. They are surrounded by ice and snow.

satellite

A satellite is a man-made object in space that circles around Earth. Satellites are sent into space to collect information and send it back to Earth.

scale

When something is drawn to scale, it is an accurate drawing that is either bigger or smaller than the real thing.

street map

A street map of a city or town shows the streets and their names or numbers and is used for finding your way around the city.

symbol

A symbol is a sign or simple picture that represents something. For example, on a map, an airplane is a symbol of an airport and a tree is a symbol of a forest.

Index